NEW Cornerstone
WORKBOOK

New Cornerstone 2
Workbook

Copyright © 2019 by Pearson Education, Inc.
All rights reserved. No part of this publication may be reproduced, stored in a retrieval system, or transmitted in any form or by any means, electronic, mechanical, photocopying, recording, or otherwise, without the prior permission of the publisher.

Pearson, 221 River Street, Hoboken, NJ 07030
Cover Credit: Max Topchii/Shutterstock

Printed in the United States of America

ISBN-13: 978-0-13-523466-2
ISBN-10: 0-13-523466-2
19 2022

www.english.com/cornerstone

Contents

Unit 1

Reading 1	Reading 2	Reading 3	Unit 1 Review
Vocabulary 3	Vocabulary 9	Vocabulary 15	Review 21
Phonics 4	Phonics 10	Phonics 16	Writing Workshop 23
Think It Over 5	Think It Over 11	Think It Over 17	Fluency 25
Grammar and Writing 7	Grammar and Writing 13	Grammar and Writing 19	Learning Checklist 27

Unit 2

Reading 1	Reading 2	Reading 3	Unit 2 Review
Vocabulary 29	Vocabulary 35	Vocabulary 41	Review 47
Phonics 30	Phonics 36	Phonics 42	Writing Workshop 49
Think It Over 31	Think It Over 37	Think It Over 43	Fluency 51
Grammar and Writing 33	Grammar and Writing 39	Grammar and Writing 45	Learning Checklist 53

Unit 3

Reading 1	Reading 2	Reading 3	Unit 3 Review
Vocabulary 55	Vocabulary 61	Vocabulary 67	Review 73
Phonics 56	Phonics 62	Phonics 68	Writing Workshop 75
Think It Over 57	Think It Over 63	Think It Over 69	Fluency 77
Grammar and Writing 59	Grammar and Writing 65	Grammar and Writing 71	Learning Checklist 79

Contents

Unit 4

Reading 1	Reading 2	Reading 3	Unit 4 Review
Vocabulary 81	Vocabulary 87	Vocabulary 93	Review 99
Phonics 82	Phonics 88	Phonics 94	Writing Workshop ... 101
Think It Over 83	Think It Over 89	Think It Over 95	Fluency 103
Grammar and Writing 85	Grammar and Writing 91	Grammar and Writing 97	Learning Checklist 105

Unit 5

Reading 1	Reading 2	Reading 3	Unit 5 Review
Vocabulary 107	Vocabulary 113	Vocabulary 119	Review 125
Phonics 108	Phonics 114	Phonics 120	Writing Workshop ... 127
Think It Over 109	Think It Over 115	Think It Over 121	Fluency 129
Grammar and Writing 111	Grammar and Writing 117	Grammar and Writing 123	Learning Checklist 131

Unit 6

Reading 1	Reading 2	Reading 3	Unit 6 Review
Vocabulary 133	Vocabulary 139	Vocabulary 145	Review 151
Phonics 134	Phonics 140	Phonics 146	Writing Workshop ... 153
Think It Over 135	Think It Over 141	Think It Over 147	Fluency 155
Grammar and Writing 137	Grammar and Writing 143	Grammar and Writing 149	Learning Checklist 157

Name _____ Date _____

Unit 1
Reading 1

Vocabulary

A. Write the word that completes each sentence.

Sight Words
- sing
- are
- buy
- eat

1. They like to _____ and clap in music class.

2. The cat and the man _____ playing.

3. I cut the grass. It is my _____.

4. I _____ my face in the morning.

5. I _____ up my messy bedroom.

Story Words
- wash
- clean
- chore

B. Circle four vocabulary words in the Word Search.

A	B	U	Y	W	A	S
S	I	N	G	E	A	T
P	X	A	R	E	M	C

3

Unit 1

Phonics

A. Write the letters in the correct order.

1.   n h d a _____

2.   m a l p _____

3.   t c a _____

4.   t h a _____

B. Write *a*, *b*, *f*, or *s* to complete each word.

5. ____ an   8. ____ ad

6. ____ nt   9. ____ ack

7. ____ at   10. ____ ct

Name _____ Date _____

Think It Over

Reread to tell about the story.

Gramps has a bag of soap. Dan can wash a sock. Dan and Gramps can wash and clean.

A. Circle the letter of the correct answer. Then write the word.

1. Dan washes a _____.

   a. car **c.** sack
   b. sock **d.** clean

2. Dan and Gramps wash and _____.

   a. clean **c.** read
   b. dance **d.** buy

3. Gramps has a bag of _____.

   a. balls **c.** soap
   b. books **d.** cans

Unit 1

B. Read the sentences. Think of the story, "Dan and Gramps." What happens first, next, and last?

Gramps can buy food.

Dan can grab a bag.

Gramps and Jan and Sam can eat.

1.

2.

3.

Name _____ Date _____

Unit 1
Reading 1

Grammar and Writing

Can + Verb

> Use **can** + verb to talk about things someone is able to do.
>
> Use **cannot** or **can't** + verb for things someone is not able to do.
>
> To ask a question, use **can** + subject + verb.

Write *can* or *can't* to complete each sentence.

1. __Can__ your sister swim? No, she __can't__.

2. _____ the baby play basketball?

   No, he _____.

3. _____ Ava ride a bike?

   Yes, she _____.

4. _____ tigers run?

   Yes, they _____.

5. _____ dogs fly?

   No, they _____.

Unit 1

Write

A. The paragraph below is missing four periods. Write the periods at the end of each sentence.

Anna likes to have fun. She can ride a bike She can also swim

Anna can't play basketball very well She cannot jump rope

B. What two things can you do? What two things can't you do? Write sentences. Use *can* and *can't*.

Unit 1
Reading 2

Name _____ Date _____

Vocabulary

A. Write the word that completes each sentence.

1. My pet _____ soft.

2. I _____ my leg.

3. Her desk is _____.

4. I _____ math in school.

5. I _____ the pen to my dad.

Sight Words
- give
- big
- feels
- hurt

Story Words
- learn
- parents
- children

B. Circle four vocabulary words in the Word Search.

E	N	P	A	R	E	N	T	S
C	H	I	L	D	R	E	N	P
Z	B	Q	T	L	E	A	R	N
U	D	F	E	E	L	S	Y	G

Unit 1

Phonics

A. Write the missing letter or letters.

1. 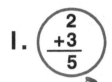 ma _____

2.  m _____ n

3.  b _____ d

4.  ba _____

5.  h _____ n

B. Write *e* or *th* to complete each word.

6. w _____ b

7. ma _____

8. n _____ t

9. _____ en

10. p _____ n

Name _____ Date _____

Think It Over

Reread to tell about the story.

Glen is a small baby. Mom and Dad help Glen. Dad can give Glen a bottle.

Glen can be fed. Then Glen can get a nap.

A. Answer the questions.

1. Who is Glen?

   _____

   _____

2. Who gives Glen a bottle?

   _____

   _____

3. What can Glen do after he has his bottle?

   _____

   _____

4. Why does Glen need a lot of care?

   _____

   _____

Unit 1

B. Match each cause with the picture that shows the effect. Write the letter of the correct answer.

1. ____ Glen can't hold his bottle.

2. ____ Bess makes a mess.

3. ____ Nell wants to eat.

4. ____ Fred has a bat.

a.

b.

c.

d.

Name _____ Date _____

Grammar and Writing

Simple Present

> Use the **simple present** to talk about things people always do. For *he*, *she*, *it*, add *-s* to the verb.
>
> For verbs ending in *ch*, *sh*, *s*, *x*, or *z*, add *-es*.
>
> For a negative, use **does not** + verb.
>
> For a Yes/No question, use **does** + subject + verb.

Write the verbs for each sentence.

1. He __watches__ TV with his family. (watch)

2. It _____ good to play outside. (feel)

3. Mr. Lin does not _____ science. (teach)

4. Sara _____ basketball every Saturday. (play)

5. _____ he wash his hands before he eats? (do)

6. A baby animal _____ from its parents. (learn)

13

Unit 1

Write

Read the sentences. Circle the error in each one. Write the correct sentences.

My dad get up early on Saturday.

He make pancakes.

We likes to go to the park.

We takes our dog.

Name _____ Date _____

Unit 1
Reading 3

Vocabulary

A. Fill in the missing letters to complete the word.

1. o w _____
2. t o w n h _____ _____ s e
3. a p a r t _____ _____ _____ _____
4. d o _____ s
5. h o u _____ _____
6. f i _____ e
7. y e _____ _____ o w

Sight Words
- yellow
- five
- does
- own

Story Words
- house
- apartment
- townhouse

B. Write the word that completes each sentence.

8. Do you have your _____ computer?
9. There are _____ people in my family.
10. Mei has a _____ backpack.

Unit 1

Phonics

A. Circle the word with the short *i* sound.

1. pin   kite
2. pine   wig
3. bit   bite
4. fish   fine

B. Draw a line to the word that names the picture.

5.    ship

6.   kick

7.   dig

8.   ill

Name _____ Date _____

Think It Over

Reread to tell about the story.

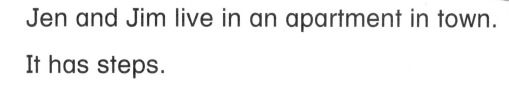

Jen and Jim live in an apartment in town. It has steps.

Jen wants a big pet, but the pet will not fit. Jim wants a fish.

A. Answer the questions.

1. Where is Jen and Jim's apartment?

   The apartment is in _____.

2. What does the apartment have?

   It has _____.

3. What does Jen want?

   Jen wants a _____.

4. What does Jim want?

   Jim wants a _____.

Unit 1

B. **Fill in the diagram. Compare and contrast your home and Jen and Jim's home. Put things that are the same in the middle. Put things that are different on one side or the other.**

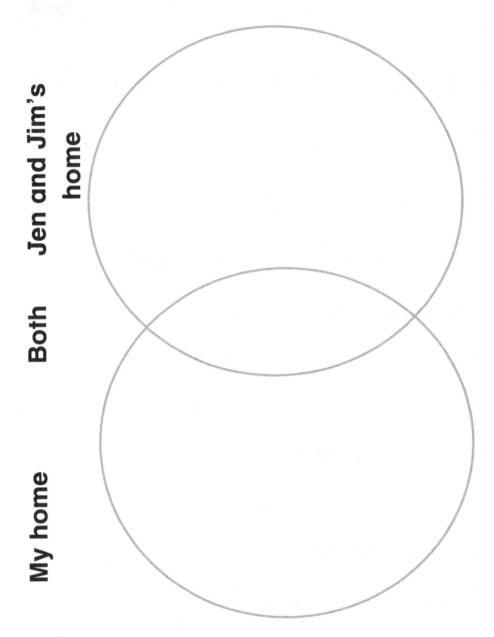

Name _____ Date _____

Grammar and Writing

Be Verbs

> The **be** verbs are **am**, **is**, and **are**.
>
> To make a negative sentence, use **am**, **is**, or **are** + **not**.
>
> To ask a question, use **Where**, **When**, or **What**, + **am**, **is**, or **are**.

A. Complete the sentences with *am*, *is*, or *are*.

1. She ____is____ my cousin.
2. We _____ at school.
3. I _____ happy today.
4. My teacher _____ nice.
5. The dogs _____ big.

Unit 1

B. Complete the sentences with a phrase from the box.

1. They ____are not____ friendly animals.
2. _____ your father?
3. Your mother _____ at home.
4. I _____ in my room.
5. _____ the green animals?

> are not
> is not
> What are
> am not
> Where is

Write

Read the paragraph. Circle the five verb errors. Write the correct words below.

Who Is Rosa?

Rosa are not my sister. She my cousin. I love my cousin Rosa. We is good friends, too. Rosa's parents be doctors. They not teachers.

1. _____
2. _____
3. _____
4. _____
5. _____

Name _____ Date _____

Review

Answer the questions after reading Unit 1. You can go back and reread to help find the answers.

1. Circle all the words with the short *a* sound.

   > Dan can grab a bag. Gramps can buy food.

2. In *Children Can Learn*, what happens because Nell is small? Circle the letter of the correct answer.

   a. She makes a mess.

   b. She takes a nap.

   c. She can get milk.

   d. She gets help from Mom.

3. Circle all the words with the short *e* sound.

   > Dad can help Bess. Bess can get milk.

Unit 1

4. Fill in the Word Web with the words for family members.

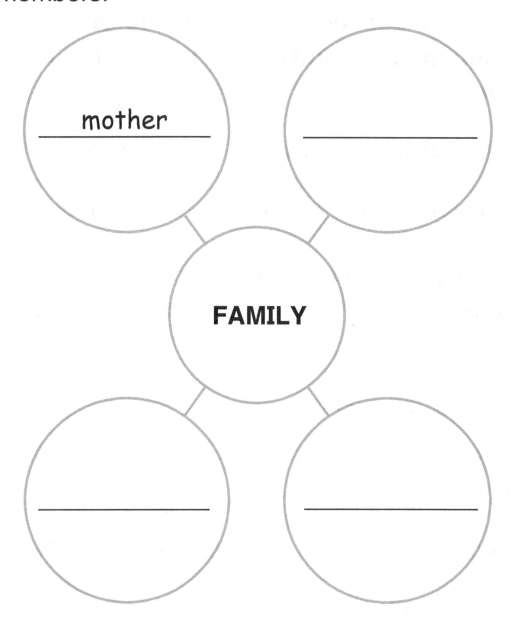

5. Circle all the words with the short *i* sound.

   Jen wants a big pet, but it will not fit.

Name _____ Date _____

Writing Workshop:
Write a Letter

Write a letter to a friend. Tell him or her what your home is like.

1. **Prewrite** Make a plan for your letter. List your ideas in the graphic organizer below.

Date _____

Dear _____,

1. _____

2. _____

3. _____

Your friend,

_____

Unit 1

2. Draft Use your plan to write a letter.

_____
_____
_____
_____
_____
_____
_____
_____

3. Revise Read your letter. Do the sentences tell about your home? Try to write better sentences.

4. Edit Use the Editing Checklist on page 58 of your book to check your work. Correct your writing.

5. Publish Make a clean copy of your letter on a separate sheet of paper. Share it with the class.

Name _____ Date _____

Fluency

A. **Take turns reading the sentences aloud with a partner. Use your finger to follow the words.**

> My apple is in the black bag.

> There is a pen on the desk.

> I think my pet fish is sick.

B. **Read the sentences in Part A again. Choose one of the sentences. Draw a picture.**

Unit 1

C. **Take turns reading the sentences aloud with a partner. Use your finger to follow the words. Read aloud for one minute. Count your words.**

Children Can Learn tells about	5
parents and how they help their	11
children learn new things. Moms and	17
Dads help feed their babies. They	23
help their children learn to spell	29
and to study for a math test. They	37
help their children with their bikes,	43
and with a bat and ball.	49

D. **Read the sentences in C to your teacher, friends, or family.**

Name _____ Date _____

Learning Checklist

Word Study and Phonics

- ☐ Two-Syllable Words
- ☐ Short *a*; Consonants
- ☐ Short *e*; *th*
- ☐ Short *i*; *sh*

Reading Strategies

- ☐ Find the Main Idea
- ☐ Cause and Effect
- ☐ Predict

Grammar

- ☐ *Can* + Verb
- ☐ Simple Present
- ☐ *Be* Verbs

Writing

- ☐ Write about what you *can* and *can't* do.
- ☐ Write about a friend or a family member.
- ☐ Write about the picture of your family.
- ☐ Writing Workshop: Write a Letter

Listening and Speaking

- ☐ Story

Name _____ Date _____

Vocabulary

A. Fill in the missing letters. Then write the word.

1. li __ h __   _____
2. f __ nn __   _____
3. y __ __ r   _____
4. hi __   _____

Sight Words
- light
- hold
- him
- funny

B. Write the word that completes each sentence.

5. I am in second grade this _____ .

6. In 15 years I will be a _____ .

7. Can you _____ my hand?

8. My little brother is a _____. He can't talk.

Story Words
- year
- baby
- grown-up

Unit 2

Phonics

A. Draw a line to the word that names the picture.

1.   fox

2.   socks

3.   pot

B. Complete each word with *o* or *wh*.

1. b ___ x
2. cl ___ ck
3. ___ at
4. ___ ale

5. ___ x
6. h ___ p
7. ___ ip
8. ___ eel

Name _____ Date _____

Think It Over

Reread to tell about the story.

This is me, Sofia. I am 14. This is my little brother, Mateo. He is eight. He is growing up fast! Soon he will be a grown-up. We are looking at pictures. It's fun! I tell him a story.

A. Answer the questions.

1. Who tells the story?
   - **a.** a baby
   - **b.** Sofia
   - **c.** a grown-up
   - **d.** Mateo

2. Who is growing up fast?

   _____

3. What do Sofia and Mateo do in the story?
   - **a.** ride a bicycle
   - **b.** look at pictures
   - **c.** ride a horse
   - **d.** grow up fast

Unit 2

B. What do Sofia and Mateo do in the story? Write their names and their ages in the boxes. Use information from the chart.

Name	Age
Sofia	14
Mateo	3
	5
	8

Action	Character	Age
read a story		
ride a tricycle		
ride a bicycle		
ride a horse		

Name _____ Date _____

Unit 2
Reading 1

Grammar and Writing

Simple Present with *I*, *You*, *We*, *They*

> Use the **simple present** to talk about facts or things that are true.
>
> To make negative statements with **I, you, we,** and **they,** use **do not** + the base form of a verb.
>
> To ask for information, use the question words **what, when,** and **where**. For **I, you, we,** and **they,** use **do** after the question word.

A. Add the verb.

1. I <u>play</u> football on Saturdays. (play)

2. Mom and I _____ cookies. (make)

3. You _____ in a house. (live)

4. I _____ music lessons. (take)

5. My parents _____ the car every week. (wash)

Unit 2

B. **Make negative statements with the sentences in Practice A. Use contractions.**

1. I <u>don't play</u> football on Saturdays. (play)
2. Mom and I _____ cookies. (make)
3. You _____ in a house. (live)
4. I _____ music lessons. (take)
5. My parents _____ the car every week. (wash)

Write

Write about how you and your family usually spend your weekends. What do you usually do? What don't you do?

_____
_____
_____
_____
_____

Unit 2
Reading 2

Name _____   Date _____

Vocabulary

A. Write the word that completes each sentence.

1. I can hear the baby _____.

2. My dog ran _____. I am sad.

3. The mother fed _____ baby.

4. We have one class _____ today.

Sight Words

her
cry
left
away

Story Words

people
beautiful
swan

B. Circle seven vocabulary words in the Word Search.

A	C	R	L	E	M	L	P	B	T	N	C	R	Y	E
P	C	F	U	L	E	F	T	O	A	E	P	S	Y	Y
A	W	A	Y	Z	M	L	P	C	A	L	S	W	A	N
B	E	A	U	T	I	F	U	L	P	E	O	P	L	E
M	C	L	R	E	H	L	P	O	E	F	A	W	A	Y
O	P	F	O	G	L	E	P	A	H	T	H	E	R	O

Unit 2

Phonics

A. Complete each word with the letter *u*. Say the word. Draw a line to its picture.

1. j ___ g

2. n ___ t

3. b ___ g

4. r ___ g

5. tr ___ ck

B. Complete each word with the letters *ch*. Draw a line to its picture.

6. lun ___

7. ___ air

Name _____ Date _____

Unit 2
Reading 2

Think It Over

Reread to tell about the story.

He is not a duckling. He is a swan! Other swans are his friends. People watch him swim and children throw bread to him. He hears them say, "The new swan is the most beautiful of all." At last he belongs.

A. Answer the questions.

1. What is the duckling now? Circle the letter of the correct answer.
    a. a duck   **c.** a swan
    b. a man   **d.** a child

2. What do people say about him?
   _____
   _____

3. How does he feel at the end of the story? Circle the letter of the correct answer.
    a. sad   **c.** thin
    b. ugly   **d.** glad

37

Unit 2

B. Write sentences to tell what happens to the ugly duckling at the beginning, middle, and end of the story.

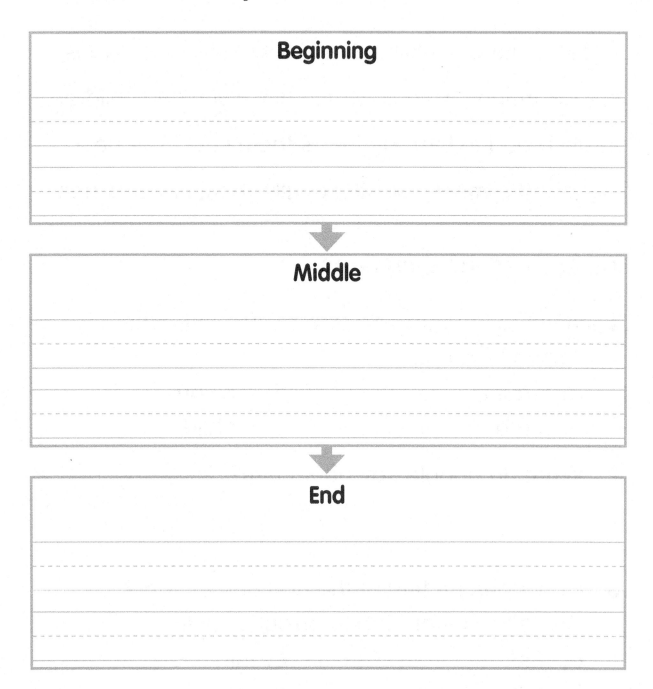

Grammar and Writing

Subject and Object Pronouns

> A pronoun can be used instead of a noun.
> Subject pronouns come before the verb.
> Object pronouns come after the verb.

Choose the correct word from the box to replace the underlined word. Rewrite the sentences.

| She | ~~He~~ | They | We | it | her | them | It |

1. <u>Dad</u> likes to sing.

   He likes to sing.

2. <u>Jim and Maria</u> draw pictures.

   _____

3. <u>Grandmother</u> reads to my brother.

   _____

4. I like <u>the new car</u>.

   _____

5. I play with <u>my sister</u>.

   _____

Unit 2

6. <u>The house</u> is red and white.

   _____

7. <u>My brother and I</u> play games.

   _____

8. I don't see <u>the children</u>.

   _____

Write

Read the sentences. Circle the error in each one. Write the correct sentences.

1. Baby chicks are little. It have fuzzy feathers.

   _____
   _____

2. The dad makes dinner. She makes them early.

   _____
   _____

3. My mom is a doctor. He works very hard.

   _____
   _____

Unit 2
Reading 3

Name _____ Date _____

Vocabulary

A. Write the letters in the right order to make a word.

Sight Words
- stay
- things
- place
- idea

1. h t e a _____
2. p l c a e _____
3. o o l c _____
4. y a t s _____
5. o p o l _____

Story Words
- heat
- pool
- cool

B. Write the word that completes each sentence.

6. I like to do many _____. I like to swim, read, eat, and play!

7. This _____ makes me hot and tired.

8. Do you want to swim at the _____?

9. It is _____ at the park under the trees.

10. I have a good _____. Listen.

41

Unit 2

Phonics

A. Complete the word.

1. c __ k __

2.  l __ k __

3. sn __ k __

4. pl __ t __

B. Circle the word with the long *a* sound.

5. lamp   lake   8. gas   gate

6. snake   snap   9. rake   rat

7. plane   plan   10. ant   ate

Name _____ Date _____

Think It Over

Reread to tell about the story.

Mom: It will be too hot to go outside today. We will have to stay indoors. We will find things to do at home.

Rosa: I do not want to stay home another day! I want to get out of the house.

Joe: What else can we do when it is so hot, Rosa? It's no fun to be outside in this heat.

A. Answer the questions. Complete each sentence.

1. What will it be like outside?

   It will be very _____.

2. Where does Mom want to stay?

   Mom wants to stay _____.

3. What does Rosa want to do?

   Rosa wants to _____

   _____.

Unit 2

B. Read each problem in the chart below. In the next column, write the solution to the problem.

Problem	Solution
1. It is too hot to go outside.	
2. Rosa and Joe do not want to stay home.	

Name _____ Date _____

Grammar and Writing

Will + Verb

> Use **will** + verb to talk about predictions and future promises. Use **will** + **not** + verb to make a negative.

A. Complete the sentences with the correct form of *will* + the verb in ().

1. We ____will visit____ you in September. (visit)

2. My brother and I _____ at the beach. (play)

3. We _____ you some chocolates! (bring)

4. I think the weather _____ perfect. (be)

5. We _____ sandwiches at the beach. (eat)

B. Complete the sentences with the negative form of *will* + the verb in (). Use contractions.

1. They ____won't stay____ home this weekend. (stay)

2. Sandra _____ TV. (watch)

Unit 2

3. I _____ you at the party. (see)

4. The cat _____ the house. (leave)

5. My family _____ at the festival. (be)

Write

Write two things you will do this summer. Write two things you won't do this summer. Use *will* and *won't*.

Name _____ Date _____

Review

Answer the questions after reading Unit 2. You can go back and reread the stories to find the answers.

1. Circle all the words with the short *o* sound. Underline the word with the *wh* sound.

   > Mateo hopped on a bicycle with two wheels.

2. What happens to Mateo in the story?

   _____
   _____

3. In *The Ugly Duckling*, who tells the duckling, "Go away!"? Circle the letter of the correct answer.

   a. his sisters　　　**c.** the other swans
   b. Mama Duck　　　**d.** the frog

4. Why do you think people watch him swim at the end of the story?

   _____
   _____
   _____

Unit 2

5. Circle the word with the short *u* sound.
Underline the word with the *ch* sound.

> We have a chore. We must clean the house.

6. What problem do Rosa and Joe have in *Fun on a Hot Day*? Circle the letter of the correct answer.

   a. They have to stay inside because of the cold weather.

   b. They have to stay inside because of the hot weather.

   c. They do not like the cold weather.

   d. They have to stay inside because of the rain.

7. How do Rosa and Joe solve their problem?

_____
_____
_____
_____

Name _____ Date _____

Unit 2

Writing Workshop:
Write to Compare and Contrast

Compare and contrast two sports or games.

1. **Prewrite** Choose two sports or games to compare. List your ideas in the graphic organizer below.

_____   **Both**   _____

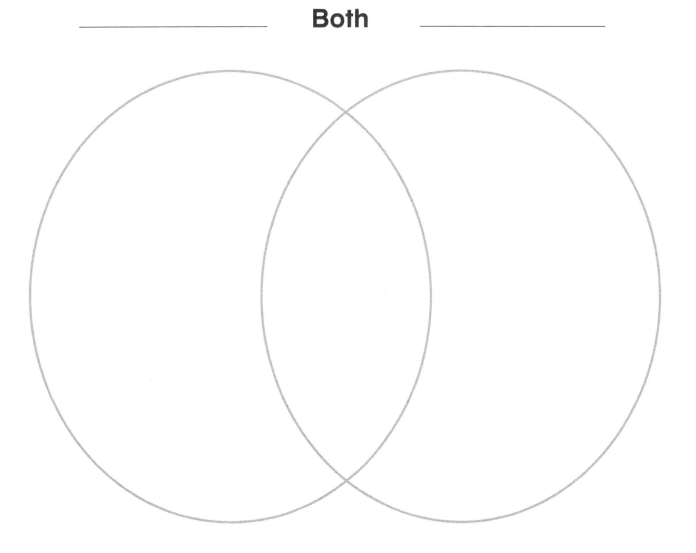

49

Unit 2

2. **Draft** Use your ideas to write a first draft.

_____
_____
_____
_____
_____
_____
_____
_____

3. **Revise** Read your draft. Does it tell how the two things are alike and different? Try to write better sentences.

4. **Edit** Use the Editing Checklist on page 114 of your book to check your work. Correct your writing.

5. **Publish** Make a clean copy of your final draft on a sheet of paper. Share it with the class.

Name _____ Date _____

Fluency

A. Take turns reading the sentences aloud with a partner. Use your finger to follow the words.

- The water in the teapot is hot.

- I forgot my lunch on the bus.

- Ann ate the whole plate of cake.

B. Read the sentences in Part A again. Choose one of the sentences. Draw a picture.

Unit 2

C. Take turns reading the sentences. Use your finger to follow the words. Read aloud for one minute. Count your words.

The Ugly Duckling tells about a mother duck and her baby	11
ducks. One duckling came from a big egg. All the other	22
baby ducks see he is not like them. They say he is ugly.	35
Duck is sad. No one plays with him. Time passes. He is a	48
beautiful swan.	50

D. Read to your teacher, friends, or family.

Name _____ Date _____

Unit 2

Learning Checklist

Word Study and Phonics

☐ Compound Words
☐ Short *o*; *wh*
☐ Short *u*; *ch*
☐ Long *a*

Reading Strategies

☐ Identify Characters
☐ Make Inferences
☐ Problem and Solution

Grammar

☐ Simple Present with *I, You, We, They*
☐ Subject and Object Pronouns
☐ *Will* + Verb

Writing

☐ Tell about yourself.
☐ Tell about an animal.
☐ Tell what you will do on the weekend.
☐ Writing Workshop: Write to Compare and Contrast

Listening and Speaking

☐ Interview

Name _____ Date _____

Unit 3
Reading 1

Vocabulary

A. Write the word that completes each sentence.

Sight Words
- special
- day
- laugh
- family

1. I love my grandma. She is a very _____ person.

2. What _____ is there no school?

3. I like to _____ with my friends.

4. My _____ has dinner together.

Story Words
- beach
- baseball
- tree

B. Fill in the missing letters to complete the word.

5. base _____
6. bea _____
7. _____ ee
8. f _____ ily
9. _____ ecial
10. la _____

55

Unit 3

Phonics

A. Write the word that names the picture.

1. _____

2.  _____

3. _____

4. _____

B. Circle the word with the long *i* sound.

5. Mike   men   8. pin   pine

6. kite   kit   9. ripe   rip

7. dinner   dime   10. time   Tim

Name _____ Date _____

Think It Over

Reread to tell about the story.

    Sam's dad takes him to a baseball game. The game is a special time. They sit in the red seats. Dad and Sam can see it all from there! Sam and his dad eat snacks. Sam jumps up to get a ball. It is a special time.

A. Answer the questions.

1. Who goes to a baseball game?

_____

_____

2. What can they see from their seats?

_____

_____

3. Why do you think this is a special time for Sam and his dad?

_____

_____

Unit 3

B. Read the words in the center circle. Think of activities that families do together. Write them in the four circles.

What Families Do Together

Name _____ Date _____

Grammar and Writing

Nouns

> A **noun** names a person, place, or thing. Use **a** or **an** to talk about one, or a singular, noun. Use *an* before a vowel.
>
> an apple → apple**s**   a box → box**es**
>
> a party → parti**es**   a beach → beach**es**
>
> a lunch → lunch**es**

A. Underline the correct word to complete the sentence.

1. I have five (present, <u>presents</u>).

2. We ate (a, an) birthday cake.

3. Many (dog, dogs) are at the park.

4. I'm going to a (party, parties).

5. The (beach, beaches) are beautiful.

6. I have (a, an) apple in my lunch bag.

Unit 3

B. Write the plural noun to complete the sentence.

1. I have <u>apples</u> for everyone! (apple)

2. Three _____ live here. (family)

3. Where are the two _____ ? (box)

4. We like to climb _____. (tree)

5. There are beautiful rose _____ in the garden. (bush)

Write

Read the paragraph. Circle the four incorrect nouns. Write the correct nouns in the list below.

Bill has a parties on his birthday. Many friend come to the party. His friends give him many present. Bill's friends play two or three game at the party.

Correct Nouns

1. _____   3. _____

2. _____   4. _____

Name _____ Date _____

Vocabulary

A. Write the word that completes each sentence.

1. Eat _____ lunch before you go outside.

2. It's a very _____ day! Please wear a hat.

3. I will give my sister the red balloon. I will _____ the blue balloon.

4. _____ wants to see a honey bee?

5. Jan can ride a _____ .

Sight Words

who
some
cold
keep

Story Words

roost
beehive
horse

B. Fill in the missing letters. Then write the word.

6. r ___ st   _____

7. hor ___   _____

8. beehi ___   _____

Unit 3

Phonics

A. Write the word that names the picture.

1. _____

2.  _____

3. _____

4. _____

B. Circle the word with the long *o* sound.

5. robe rob

6. globe glob

7. bone bond

8. cane cone

9. hose hot

10. poke plop

11. hop hope

12. home horse

Name _____ Date _____

Think It Over

Reread to tell about the story.

Who woke up? Joe woke up. Joe is getting an egg from a hen. The hens are roosting in nests. Joe is getting lots of eggs. He will keep some eggs, and he will sell some eggs.

A. Answer the questions.

1. What did Joe get from the hen?
   He got an _____ .

2. What will Joe do with the eggs?
   He will _____ some and he will _____ some.

3. Why do you think the hens roost in nests?
   Hens roost in nests because nests are _____ .

Unit 3

B. Read the sentences. Complete the chart for Kate, Jane, and Jan.

What They Like
Joe likes to get up in the morning.
Kate likes to check on her beehives.
Jane likes to milk her cow, Bell.
Jan likes her horse, Rose.

Why They Like It
Joe likes to gather eggs from his hens.
Kate _____ _____ .
Jane _____ _____ .
Jan _____ _____ .

Name _____ Date _____

Unit 3
Reading 2

Grammar and Writing

Present Progressive: *be* + *-ing*

> Use the **present progressive** to talk about things that are or are not happening now.
>
> I **am sitting** in my room.
>
> I **am not watching** TV right now.
>
> I **am reading** a good book.
>
> To make a present progressive statement negative, add *not* after *is, am,* and *are*.

Complete each sentence with the present progressive form of the verb in ( ).

1. I <u>am getting</u> a snack. (get)
2. He _____ to his dad. (talk)
3. They _____ in the classroom. (sit)
4. We _____ fun! (have)
5. My sister _____ cookies. Yum! (bake)
6. The family _____ TV. (watch)

Unit 3

7. I _____ to school today. (not go)

8. The bunny _____ up and down! (hop)

9. We _____ a test today. (not take)

Write

The paragraph below has four errors. Circle the errors. Rewrite the paragraph.

I am watch my cat. She isn't sleep. She runs. She is have fun!

Name _____ Date _____

Vocabulary

A. Circle five vocabulary words in the Word Search.

S	W	E	D	R	M
D	J	F	O	M	I
O	B	A	W	H	D
N	K	O	N	E	D
E	P	S	H	U	L
S	B	A	L	L	E

Sight Words
we
done
ball
down

Story Words
kick
soccer
middle

B. Write the word or words that complete each sentence.

8. Let's sit _____ when we are _____.

9. Paco can _____ the _____.

10. Stand in the _____ of the circle.

11. Now _____ are listening to music.

12. Do you like to watch _____?

Unit 3

Phonics

A. Circle the word with the long *u* sound.

1. cute   cut
2. June   gum
3. cub   cube
4. use   under
5. uncle   uniform

B. Draw a line to the word that names the picture.

6.    cube

7.    mule

8. 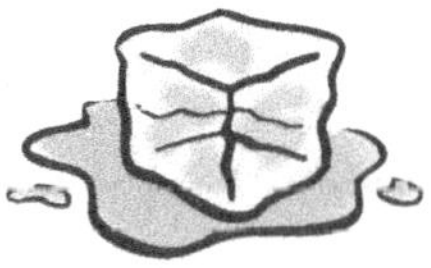   use

Name _____ Date _____

Think It Over

Reread to tell about the story.

County Fairs
Occur in June
They are great fun
But end too soon.

Go on rides
Eat treats by the heap
Then say good-bye
To get some sleep.

A. Answer the questions.

1. What happens in June?

   _____

2. What do people eat at the county fair?

   _____

3. Why do you think the author says county fairs end too soon?

   _____

Unit 3

B. Look at the pictures. Fill in the chart with words that name fun things to do.

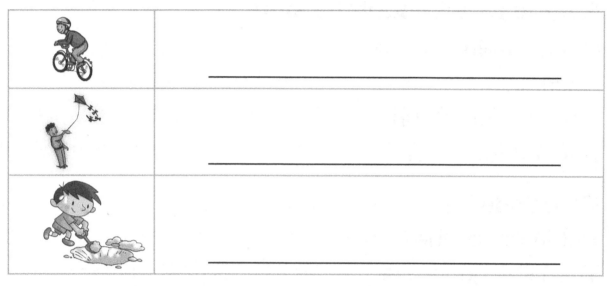

Draw a picture of something you would like to do and play.

Name _____ Date _____

Grammar and Writing

Adjectives

> An adjective describes a noun or pronoun. It can go before a noun. An adjective can also follow **be** (*am, is, are*).

A. Look at each set of words. Underline the adjectives.

B. Now unscramble the words to make sentences. Write the sentences on the lines.

1. The / wet / towel / is.

   The towel is wet.

2. My / are / fun / friends!

3. It's / bicycle / red / a.

4. She / chocolate / likes / ice cream.

Unit 3 Reading 3

71

Unit 3

5. That / is / big / elephant!

Write

Read the sentences. Circle the error in each one. Write the correct sentences.

I have hair black.

My best friend tall is.

We brown have eyes.

Wild animals awesome are!

Name _____ Date _____

Review

Answer the questions after reading Unit 3. You can reread the stories to find the answers.

1. Circle all the words with the long *i* sound.

   > It is time to fly my kite. I will have fun.

2. In *A Special Time*, what do Sam and his dad do at the baseball game?

   _____
   _____

3. Who likes to hike?

   _____ like to hike.

4. In *Who Woke Up?*, why do you think Joe keeps some eggs?

   _____
   _____
   _____
   _____

Unit 3

5. Circle all the words with the long *o* sound.

> We pet Rose on her soft nose.

6. Circle all the words with the long *u* sound.

> They use mules to help them work.

7. In *Playing Games*, what activity does the author NOT talk about? Circle the letter of the correct answer.

a. playing soccer   **c.** riding horses

b. eating treats   **d.** jumping in hay

8. What do you like to do with your friends, family, or on your own? Write two or three sentences.

_____

_____

_____

_____

Name _____ Date _____

Writing Workshop:
Write a Descriptive Paragraph

You will write a paragraph describing a holiday.

1. **Prewrite** Choose a holiday to describe. List your ideas in the graphic organizer below.

I see	I hear	I taste

Unit 3

2. **Draft** Use your ideas to write a first draft.

_____
_____
_____
_____
_____
_____
_____
_____
_____
_____

3. **Revise** Read your draft. Do the sentences describe the holiday? Try to write better sentences.

4. **Edit** Use the Editing Checklist on page 174 of your book to check your work. Correct your writing.

5. **Publish** Make a clean copy of your final draft on a sheet of paper. Share it with the class.

Name _____ Date _____

Fluency

A. Take turns reading the sentences aloud with a partner. Use your finger to follow the words.

- It's time to play on the slide!

- My dog dug a hole for his bone.

- Do you like to play music?

B. Read the sentences in Part A again. Choose one of the sentences. Draw a picture.

Unit 3

C. Take turns reading the sentences. Use your finger to follow the words. Read aloud for one minute. Count your words.

"Who Woke Up?" tells about people	6
and the things they do in the morning.	14
Bob gets eggs. Mike and Jim eat eggs	22
and bread. Kate gets honey from bees.	29
Jane gets a pail of milk from Bell.	37
The cow eats hay. Jan rides her horse.	45
Children pet the horse. Kids laugh and	52
joke and have a good time.	58

D. Read to your teacher, friends, or family.

Name _____ Date _____

Unit 3

Learning Checklist

Word Study and Phonics

- ☐ Antonyms and Synonyms
- ☐ Long *i*
- ☐ Long *o*
- ☐ Long *u*

Reading Strategies

- ☐ Author's Purpose
- ☐ Find Details
- ☐ Use Prior Knowledge

Grammar

- ☐ Nouns
- ☐ Present Progressive: *be* + *-ing*
- ☐ Adjectives

Writing

- ☐ Describe what you do on your birthday.
- ☐ Describe what a classmate is doing.
- ☐ Describe an object.
- ☐ Writing Workshop: Write a Descriptive Paragraph

Listening and Speaking

- ☐ Description Game

Name _____ Date _____

Unit 4
Reading 1

Vocabulary

A. Write the word that completes each sentence.

Sight Words
- friends
- roads
- very
- letter

Story Words
- simple
- email
- board

1. A word that means "streets" is _____ .

2. I invited my _____ to a party.

3. That is a _____ question. Even my little brother can answer it.

4. I like strawberries _____ much.

5. I use the computer to write an _____ to my grandma.

B. Write the letters in the correct order to make a word.

6. r e f i s d n   _____

7. r o b a d   _____

8. t e l e r t   _____

81

Unit 4

Phonics

A. Write *ai* or *ay* to complete each word.

1.   tr ____ n

2.   pl ____

3.   sn ____ l

4.   r ____ n

B. Write *th* or *ch* to complete each word.

5.   ____ ree

6.   pea ____

7.   ba ____

8.   ____ alk

Name _____ Date _____

Think It Over

Reread to tell about the story.

A long time ago, we drove on roads that had a lot of rocks and bumps. A horse led the way. We used a stick and a rope to tell the horse which way to go. We pulled the rope to say, "Stop!"

A. Answer the questions.

1. How were roads in the past?
   _____
   _____

2. How did the horse know which way to go?
   _____
   _____

3. Why do you think the roads were full of rocks and bumps?
   _____
   _____

Unit 4

B. Complete the KWL Chart. In the first column, write about how people lived long ago. Write what you want to know in the middle column. In the last column, write what you learned.

K- What I Know	W- What I Want to Know	L- What I Learned
_____	_____	_____
_____	_____	_____
_____	_____	_____
_____	_____	_____
_____	_____	_____
_____	_____	_____
_____	_____	_____

Name _____ Date _____

Unit 4
Reading 1

Grammar and Writing

Simple Past Tense: Regular Verbs

> Use the **past tense** to talk about events that happened in the past.
>
> Add **-ed** to the main verb to form the past tense.
>
> Use **did not** or **didn't** + the base form of the verb to form the negative past tense.

Choose a word from the box to complete the sentence. Write the past tense of the verb.

1. Mom ____walked____ to the store.
2. Dad _____ dinner last night.
3. We _____ to music.
4. My friends _____ soccer over the weekend.
5. Marcus _____ at my joke.
6. I _____ to read last year.

| play |
| laugh |
| ~~walk~~ |
| cook |
| listen |
| learn |

85

Unit 4

Write

Write four sentences about things you did and didn't do yesterday.

Example: I walked to school yesterday.
I didn't cook dinner yesterday.

Name _____ Date _____

Vocabulary

A. Write the word that matches the clue.

1. opposite of bad   _____
2. not this one   _____
3. opposite of far   _____
4. you have no doubt   _____

Sight Words
- near
- sure
- good
- other

B. Write the word that completes each sentence.

5. Ice cream is a special _____ .
6. A _____ cone holds a lot of ice cream.
7. Berries make a _____ dessert.

Story Words
- tasty
- treat
- waffle

Unit 4

Phonics

A. Circle the words with the long *e* sound.

> Ice cream is a cold and sweet treat.

B. Draw a line to the word that names the picture.

1.   sleep

2.   read

3.   peach

4.   meat

5.   leaf

Name _____ Date _____

Think It Over

Reread to tell about the story.

A big fair was held in 1904. The sun was bright and high in the clear, blue sky. A lot of kids and adults came to play and have fun. They were hot. They ate a lot of ice cream.

A. Answer the questions.

1. Why were the people hot?
   _____
   _____

2. Why do you think people like to eat ice cream?
   _____
   _____

3. Draw a picture of a fair.

Unit 4

B. Write words that tell about ice cream.

Name _____ Date _____

Grammar and Writing

Past *Be*

> Use the past forms of **be** to talk about the past.
>
> Use **was** with *I, he, she,* and *it*.
>
> Use **were** with *you, we,* and *they*.
>
> Use **was not** or **were not** for negative sentences.

Write *was* or *were* to complete the sentence.

1. Our lunch ____was____ good.
2. The dog _____ hurt.
3. Mom and Dad _____ happy.
4. The music _____ loud.
5. The pool water _____ cold.
6. The cookies _____ good.

Unit 4

Write

Write four sentences about the picture. Use *was*, *were*, *wasn't*, **and** *weren't*.

Example: The day *was* warm.

Name _____ Date _____

Vocabulary

A. Write the letters in the correct order to make a word.

1. m s e a _____
2. m a n l a i _____
3. o t h u c _____

Sight Words

animal
same
touch

B. Draw a line to match each word with its clue.

Story Words

scientist
outdoors
legacy
protect

4. outdoors   a. This is to keep safe from danger.

5. legacy   b. This is not in a building.

6. scientist   c. This is something handed down to others.

7. protect   d. This is someone who works in science.

Unit 4

Phonics

A. Circle the words with the long *i* or the soft *g* sound.

1. The lights are bright tonight.
2. Sam flies his kite at the beach.
3. I wrote nine sentences on the page.
4. My sister sang the song on a stage.
5. Jim has a very nice smile.

B. Complete the word that names the picture.

6. n ____ t

7. sl ____ de

8. sk ____

9.  ____ ie

Name _____ Date _____

Think It Over

Read to tell about the story.

Today, Jane Goodall's legacy lives on. Scientists around the world continue her work. They work to protect animals. They also work to protect the outdoors, where animals live. And we can all enjoy her many books!

A. Answer the questions.

1. How do scientists continue Goodall's work?

   _____
   _____
   _____
   _____

2. What can everyone enjoy?

   _____
   _____
   _____
   _____

Unit 4

B. **Think about Jane Goodall's life. Number the events from 1–4 to show the order that they happened.**

_____ She met Dr. Louis Leakey.

_____ She studied chimpanzees.

_____ She sailed on a ship to Africa.

_____ She had a dream to study animals in Africa.

Name _____ Date _____

Grammar and Writing

Past Tense: Irregular Verbs

> Do not add **-ed** to irregular verbs. The past form of irregular verbs varies.

> Use **did not** or **didn't** + the base form of the verb to form the negative past tense of irregular verbs.

Complete the sentences with the base form of the verb or the past tense form of the verb.

1. Last summer, I _____ (go) to visit my grandmother.

2. We _____ (eat) waffles with fruit for breakfast.

3. I didn't _____ (go) to school because it was summertime.

4. My cousin _____ (come) to visit my grandmother, too.

Unit 4

5. Every day, we _____ (sleep) late and visited the beach.

6. We _____ (see) fish at the beach.

7. We didn't _____ (see) any ships at the beach.

Write

Write four sentences about Jane Goodall's life. Here are some questions to help you: How old was she when she sailed to Africa? Who did she meet in Africa? What animals did she study? What did she write?

_____
_____
_____
_____
_____
_____
_____
_____

Unit 4

Name _____ Date _____

Review

Answer the questions after reading Unit 4. Go back and reread if you need help.

1. Circle all the words with the long *a* sound.

   > Then she put it in the mail. A letter may take days to get to a friend.

2. What couldn't be done in the past? Circle the letter of the correct answer.
   - **a.** play chess
   - **b.** travel to another city
   - **c.** send an email
   - **d.** wash clothes

3. Circle all the words with the long *e* sound.

   > We eat ice cream when we go to the beach.

4. In *Ice Cream Cones*, what did the ice cream man run out of? Circle the letter of the correct answer.
   - **a.** dishes
   - **b.** cones
   - **c.** ice cream
   - **d.** spoons

Unit 4

5. Why do you think kids still eat ice cream today?

_____

_____

_____

_____

6. How did Jane Goodall get close to chimpanzees? Circle the letter of the correct answer.

    a. She acted like a chimpanzee.

    b. She sat in a tree.

    c. She ate the same food as the chimpanzees.

    d. All of the above.

7. Do you think Jane Goodall's dreams came true? Why or why not?

_____

_____

_____

_____

_____

_____

_____

Name _____ Date _____

Unit 4

Writing Workshop:
Write a Story

Write a story about something that happened a long time ago. It can be a true story or one that you make up.

1. Prewrite Plan your story. Use the chart to help.

Who is in the story? Write the names of the characters.	Where does it happen? Write the time and the place.
What problem does the main character have?	How is the problem solved?

Unit 4

2. **Draft** Use your chart to write a first draft.

   _____
   _____
   _____
   _____
   _____
   _____
   _____
   _____
   _____
   _____

3. **Revise** Read your draft. Do the sentences tell about the story? Try to write better sentences.

4. **Edit** Use the Editing Checklist on page 232 of your book to check your work. Correct your writing.

5. **Publish** Make a clean copy of your story on a sheet of paper. Share it with the class.

Name _____ Date _____

Unit 4

Fluency

A. Take turns reading the sentences aloud with a partner. Use your finger to follow the words.

- I got an email from my sister today.

- The last leaf fell from the tree.

- I like to bake apple cake.

B. Read the sentences in Part A again. Choose one of the sentences. Draw a picture.

Unit 4

C. Take turns reading the sentences aloud with a partner. Use your finger to follow the words. Read aloud for one minute. Count your words.

D. Read to your teacher, friends, or family.

Ice Cream Cones tells how a tasty treat we	9
love to eat came to be. At a big fair on a hot	22
day in 1904, a man ran out of dishes to put	33
his scoops of ice cream in. He still had lots	43
of ice cream to sell. A waffle man helped	52
him make cone shapes for the ice cream.	60

Name _____ Date _____

Unit 4

Learning Checklist

Word Study and Phonics

☐ Multiple-Meaning Words
☐ Long *a*; *ch*, *th*
☐ Long *e*
☐ Long *i*; soft *g*

Reading Strategies

☐ Draw Conclusions
☐ Summarize
☐ Ask Questions

Grammar

☐ Simple Past Tense: Regular Verbs
☐ Past *Be*
☐ Past Tense: Irregular Verbs

Writing

☐ Write about your day.
☐ Tell about your weekend.
☐ Tell about the life of someone in your family.
☐ Writing Workshop: Write a Story

Listening and Speaking

☐ Skit

Name _____ Date _____

Unit 5
Reading 1

Vocabulary

A. Write the word that completes each sentence.

1. A _____ runs across the yard.

2. She _____ on a nut.

3. I ate a big _____ apple for a snack.

4. I planted a _____ tree with my dad.

Sight Words

have
small
found

Story Words

squirrel
nibbles
delicious

B. Circle three vocabulary words in the Word Search.

S	U	L	Q	A	F
M	H	A	V	E	O
A	T	B	T	G	U
L	C	A	L	L	N
L	M	P	U	O	D

107

Unit 5

Phonics

A. Write the word that names the picture.

1. _____

2. _____

3.  _____

4. _____

B. Draw a line to the word that names the picture.

5.   stage

6.   blow

7.   gem

8.   page

Name _____ Date _____

Think It Over

Reread to tell about the story.

    A nest with eggs sits high in this tree. Twigs, twine, and trash make up this nest. Mother bird will wait till her chicks grow in the eggs. Small chicks will poke holes and crack the shells. Then Mother will find a meal her chicks can eat.

A. Answer the questions.

1. What makes up the nest? Circle the answer.
   - **a.** leaves
   - **b.** twigs, twine, and trash
   - **c.** feathers
   - **d.** a tree

2. What is Mother bird waiting for?

   She is waiting for _____ .

3. How do the chicks get out of the eggs?

   The chicks _____ .

Unit 5

B. Read each sentence. Write the number of each Cause next to its Effect.

CAUSE	EFFECT
1. The bird sits on her eggs.	____ A fly gets stuck.
2. The spider spins a web.	____ It will have food for winter.
3. The bird catches a worm.	____ The chicks hatch.
4. The squirrel piles up nuts at home.	____ The chick can eat.

Name _____ Date _____

Grammar and Writing

Prepositions of Location

> *In*, *on*, *at*, *next to*, *under*, and *between* are prepositions of location. They tell the location of places and things. Use prepositions of location to answer questions with *where*.

Look at the photo. Circle the correct preposition of location to complete the sentence.

1. The Olivos family is **at / in** home.

2. The family is doing homework **in / on** the dining room.

3. The dad is sitting **next to / between** the girl.

4. The mom is sitting **between / under** the boy and the girl.

5. The notebooks are **on / between** the table.

111

Unit 5

6. The family's feet are **under / on** the table.

7. There are pencils **on / next to** the table.

Write

Read the sentences. Write an answer to each question.

1. Where do you do your homework?

2. Where do you eat breakfast every day?

3. Where is your best friend now?

4. Where do you put your bag at home?

Name _____ Date _____

Vocabulary

A. Write the word that completes each sentence.

Sight Words
- was
- said
- soon
- water

1. My dad _____ he would arrive early.

2. I can reach the shelf when I stretch my _____ up.

3. I like to play in the water by the _____ .

4. It _____ sunny when I got up.

5. _____ is my favorite drink.

Story Words
- arms
- shore
- sign

B. Circle the vocabulary words.

6. "We will go to the beach soon," my mom said.

7. The sign on the shore said, "Keep out of the water."

Unit 5

Phonics

A. Write the word that names the picture.

1.		_____
2.		_____
3.		_____
4.		_____

soup

new

glue

screw

B. Circle the words with the same sound as the *ue* in *clue*.

5. I ate fruit and soup.

6. I have a new blue coat.

7. We knew it was a true story.

8. Ed drew a picture of Sue.

Name _____ Date _____

Think It Over

Reread to tell about the story.

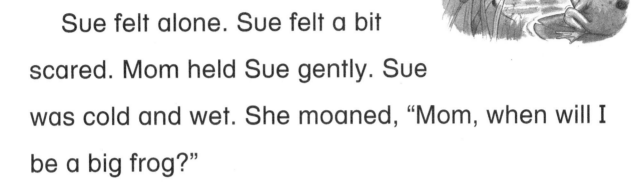

Sue felt alone. Sue felt a bit scared. Mom held Sue gently. Sue was cold and wet. She moaned, "Mom, when will I be a big frog?"

Mom said, "Soon. It is true. You will be a big frog in a few weeks."

A. Answer the questions.

1. Who is Sue?

   Sue is a _____.

2. How did she feel?

   Sue felt _____.

3. What was Sue's problem?

   Sue wanted _____.

Unit 5

B. Write what happened to Sue in the beginning, middle, and end of the story.

Beginning

Middle

End

Name _____ Date _____

Unit 5
Reading 2

Grammar and Writing

Adverbs of Manner

> An adverb describes the action of a verb.
> Add **-ly** to an adjective to make some adverbs.
> **Well** is the adverb form of **good**.

Complete each sentence with the adverb form of the word in ( ).

1. We talked <u>quietly</u>. (quiet)
2. The team cheered _____. (loud)
3. We cleaned up _____. (quick)
4. Please write _____. (neat)
5. The hikers walked _____. (careful)
6. The birds sang _____. (sweet)
7. She speaks English very _____. (good)
8. We write in our notebooks _____. (clear)

Unit 5

9. The turtle moves _____ . (slow)

Write

Complete the paragraph with adverbs. Use the words in parentheses.

The teacher speaks _____ and _____ . (slow; clear)

She speaks English very _____ . (good)

The students work _____ at their desks. (quiet)

I always listen _____ . (careful)

I want to learn English _____ . (quick)

Name _____ Date _____

Vocabulary

A. Fill in the letter or letters to complete each word.

Sight Words
- ground
- air
- more
- many

1. a i ___
2. h ___ b ___ t ___ t
3. m ___ r ___
4. m ___ n ___
5. n ___ t ___ r ___
6. g r ___ ___ n d
7. e ___ o s y s ___ e m

Story Words
- ecosystem
- nature
- habitat

B. Write the word that completes each sentence.

8. The owl's _____ is in the rainforest.

9. I like to take walks in _____. I especially like the forest.

10. Let's find rocks on the _____.

Unit 5 Reading 3

Unit 5

Phonics

A. Circle the word with the same *ow* sound as in *clown*.

1. row   gown
2. crowd   throw
3. flower   snow
4. cow   blow

B. Write the word with *ou* that names the picture.

5. _____

6.  _____

7. _____

8. _____

Name _____   Date _____

Unit 5
Reading 3

Think It Over

Reread to tell about the story.

The clownfish likes to live on coral reefs. Their home, or habitat, on the reef is in anemones. The clownfish clean the anemones, and the anemones protect the clownfish. Some people call clownfish anemonefish!

A. Answer the questions.

1. What is the clownfish's habitat?
   _____

2. How do clownfish help anemones?
   _____

3. How do anemones help clownfish?
   _____

Unit 5

B. Complete the KWL Chart. In the first column, write one thing you already knew about plants and animals in different ecosystems. In the middle column, write one question you wanted to know. In the last column, write one thing you learned.

K- What I Knew	W- What I Wanted to Know	L- What I Learned
_____	_____	_____
_____	_____	_____
_____	_____	_____
_____	_____	_____
_____	_____	_____
_____	_____	_____

Name _____ Date _____

Grammar and Writing

Possessives and Possessive Pronouns

> Use the possessive form **'s** to show that someone owns something.
>
> Use an apostrophe (') to form the possessive of plural nouns that end in *-s*.
>
> Use a possessive adjective before a noun.
>
> Use a possessive pronoun in place of a noun.

A. Complete the sentence with the possessive form of the noun in parentheses.

1. It is my _____ book. (brother)
2. The _____ artwork is on the classroom wall. (students)
3. That is my _____ car. (father)
4. This is the _____ food. (animals)
5. It is my _____ backpack. (friend)

Unit 5

B. Complete the sentences with a possessive adjective or a possessive pronoun.

1. It's her bike. It's _____ .

2. It's _____ book. It is yours.

3. It is my room. It's _____ .

4. It's _____ house. It is ours.

5. It's their team. It is _____ .

Write

Read the paragraph. Circle the four errors. Write the correct word above each error.

(Mine) sister Meera has a new car. Meera car is red. She car has soft seats. Its car has a CD player, too. Meera and I drive to we favorite park on Saturdays.

My

Name _____ Date _____

Review

Answer the questions after reading Unit 5. You can go back and reread to help find the answers.

1. Circle all the words with the long *o* sound.

   > Some squirrels roam around and make homes in trees.

2. What does the spider eat? Circle the letter of the correct answer.
   - **a.** an egg
   - **b.** a chick
   - **c.** an insect
   - **d.** nuts

3. In *Sue the Tadpole*, what can Sue do at the beginning of the story? Circle the letter of the correct answer.
   - **a.** swim
   - **b.** jump
   - **c.** hop
   - **d.** run

4. In *Sue the Tadpole*, why does Sue say that it was worth waiting for arms and legs?

   _____

   _____

Unit 5

5. Circle the words with the same sound as the *ue* in *blue*.

> Sue was sad. Mom said, "Soon. It is true. You will be a big frog in a few weeks."

6. Describe the ecosystem where the desert mouse lives.

_____

_____

_____

7. Circle the words with the same sound you hear in *clown*.

> The brown desert mouse stays underground. It doesn't make a sound.

8. Write two things you learned in this unit.

_____

_____

_____

_____

Name _____ Date _____

Writing Workshop
Write a Description

Write a description of a room.

1. **Prewrite** Plan your description. List your ideas in the chart below.

I see . . .	I hear . . .
I smell . . .	**I feel . . .**

Unit 5

Unit 5

2. **Draft** Use your chart to write a first draft.

3. **Revise** Read your draft. Can a reader picture what you describe? Try to write better sentences.

4. **Edit** Use the Editing Checklist on page 292 of your book to check your work. Correct your writing.

5. **Publish** Make a clean copy of your description on a sheet of paper. Share it with the class.

Name _____ Date _____

Unit 5

Fluency

A. Read the sentences aloud. Practice saying them as fast as you can with no mistakes.

1. George saw a goat eating rope on a boat.

2. The group got new spoons and soon ate all the soup.

3. The clown found a mouse in his big brown house.

B. Read each sentence several times. Then cover each one with your hand and try to say it word for word.

1. Birds make nests and spiders make webs in trees.

2. A fat little tadpole grows up to be a loud frog.

3. The desert ecosystem has very dry land.

Unit 5

C. Take turns reading the sentences aloud with a partner. Use your finger to follow the words. Read aloud for one minute. Count your words.

Sue the Tadpole tells the story of a	8
baby tadpole who wants to be a big frog	17
fast. She feels alone and scared. Her	24
mom and dad say she will grow in a few	34
weeks. Sue wants to jump and hop from	42
leaf to leaf in the pond right now. She	51
waits and waits. Time passes, and Sue	58
gets arms and legs. She gets a prize in	67
a jumping show.	70

D. Read to your teacher, friends, or family.

Name _____ Date _____

Learning Checklist

Word Study and Phonics

- ☐ Prefixes
- ☐ Long *o*; soft *g*
- ☐ Letters: *ew, ou*
- ☐ Letters: *ow, ou*

Reading Strategies

- ☐ Cause and Effect
- ☐ Sequence of Events
- ☐ Make Inferences

Grammar

- ☐ Prepositions of Location
- ☐ Adverbs of Manner
- ☐ Possessives and Possessive Pronouns

Writing

- ☐ Describe a room in your home.
- ☐ Describe how an animal moves.
- ☐ Write what you and your partner talked about.
- ☐ Writing Workshop: Write a Description

Listening and Speaking

- ☐ Speech

Name _____ Date _____

Unit 6
Reading 1

Vocabulary

A. Write the word that completes each sentence.

Sight Words
- around
- world
- warm

1. I like _____ weather.

2. We eat _____ from our garden. I like carrots best.

3. Let's take a walk _____ the pond.

4. There are many different cultures in the _____ .

Story Words
- vegetables
- cabbage
- tofu

B. Circle the vocabulary words.

5. All kinds of vegetables grow around the world.

6. We ate warm tofu for lunch.

133

Unit 6

Phonics

A. Write *ir*, *ur*, or *er* to complete each word.

1.  b _____ d

2. n _____ se

3. g _____ l

4. sh _____ t

B. Circle the word that has the same *-r* sound as in *girl*.

5. date	dirt	10. birth	bark
6. purr	play	11. first	fire
7. nerve	nest	12. her	here
8. fur	far	13. bride	firm
9. burn	born	14. stir	stick

Name _____ Date _____

Unit 6
Reading 1

Think It Over

Reread to tell about the story.

My name is Bea. I have a new friend. His name is Anh. Every Saturday, Anh comes to my house to play and eat dinner. We have spaghetti and meatballs with tomato sauce and warm bread. We like to put cheese on the spaghetti. It's delicious! We eat with forks and knives.

A. Answer the questions.

1. When does Anh go to Bea's house?
   _____
   _____

2. What do Bea and Anh do?
   _____
   _____

3. What kind of sauce do they like to eat with spaghetti and meatballs?
   _____
   _____

Unit 6

B. Write a sentence to answer each question about Italy and Vietnam.

My Friend From Vietnam
Who is Bea's friend?
Where is Vietnam?
What is an example of Italian food?
When do Bea and Anh eat Italian food?
Why does Bea want to make corn pudding?

Name _____ Date _____

Grammar and Writing

Infinitive

> An infinitive consists of **to** + the base form of the verb. Use infinitives after **want**, **like**, and **would like**.
>
> For negative statements, use **doesn't/don't like to** + the infinitive.

A. Complete the sentences with the infinitive verb.

1. Bea and Anh like <u>to study</u> English. (study)

2. They like _____ dinner together. (eat)

3. Anh would like _____ fruit and chocolate cake every day! (have)

4. Anh eats dessert quickly. He doesn't want _____ . (stop)

5. Bea would like _____ sweet corn pudding for her family. (make)

137

Unit 6

B. Complete the paragraph below with infinitives from the box.

Vietnam is a country in Asia. I would like _____ Vietnam. I don't want _____ noodle soup with a knife and fork. I want _____ chopsticks. But first I would like _____ the Vietnamese words for *Hello* and *Thank you*.

| to use |
| to visit |
| to learn |
| to eat |

Write

Would you like to visit Vietnam or Italy? Choose one country. Write what you would like to do there.

_____
_____
_____
_____
_____
_____
_____

Name _____ Date _____

Unit 6
Reading 2

Vocabulary

A. Circle four vocabulary words in the Word Search.

S	W	E	D	R	B
W	O	U	L	D	E
O	O	H	W	H	T
U	N	D	E	R	T
L	L	S	H	U	E
D	Y	A	V	L	R

Sight Words
- would
- better
- only
- under

Story Words
- continent
- students

B. Write the word that completes each sentence.

1. I like milk _____ than orange juice.

2. There are eighteen _____ in my class.

3. Asia is a big _____ .

4. Look _____ the chair for the cat.

139

Unit 6

Phonics

A. Write the word that names the picture.

		car
		farm
		barn
		stars

1.  _____

2.   _____

3.  _____

4.   _____

B. Write the letter or letters to complete each word.

5.   ____ m

6.  ____ ark

7.   ____ arden

8.   ____ ard

Name _____ Date _____

Unit 6
Reading 2

Think It Over

Reread to tell about the story.

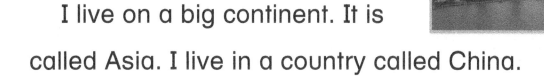

I live on a big continent. It is called Asia. I live in a country called China.

My flag has only two colors. It is red with yellow stars. One star is big. The other stars are not big.

A. Answer the questions.

1. Where does this boy live?
   a. Europe   c. Africa
   b. Asia   d. Australia

2. What colors are on the flag of China?
   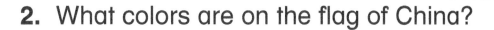

3. Look at the flag. How many big stars are on the flag? _____
   How many small stars are on the flag?
   _____

Unit 6

B. Think of the place where you live. Think of what you learned about food and eating in Italy. Put things that are alike in the middle. Put things that are different on one side or the other.

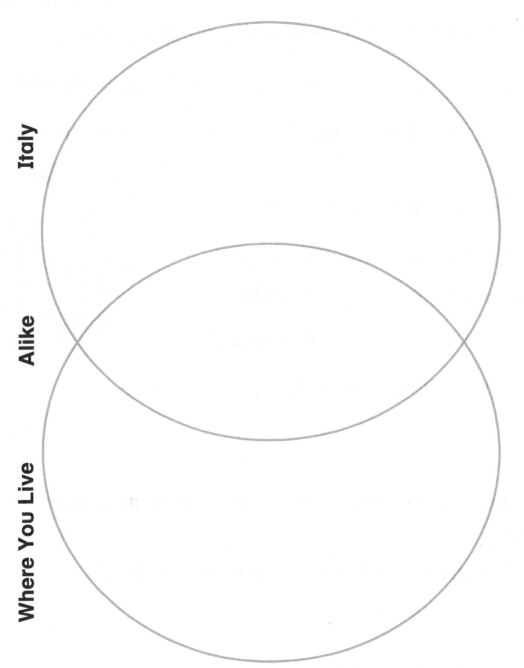

Name _____ Date _____

Grammar and Writing

Capitalization

> Use capitals for proper nouns.
>
> Use capitals for names of days of the week, months, and holidays. Do not use capitals for the names of the seasons.

A. Underline the proper nouns in each sentence.

I would like to visit California in the United States this summer. California is a very big state. I would like to hike in the mountains with my friend Darius. I could also swim in the Pacific Ocean. I would also like to visit Joshua Tree National Park in the desert.

Unit 6

B. Circle the capitalization mistakes in the sentences below.

1. My brother's birthday is in november.

2. It is cold in london in the Winter.

3. My favorite holiday is international children's day.

4. I like to go to pacific beach in the summer.

5. Will you go to school on saturday?

Write

Read the paragraph. Circle the six words that should start with a capital letter. Correct them.

    I
italy is a country in europe. People there speak italian. My family and I go to florence, italy, every summer. We like to eat spaghetti and meatballs. My brother and I like to play in cascine park.

Vocabulary

A. Fill in the missing vowels to complete each word.

1. m ___ rn ___ ng
2. c ___ ___ ntry
3. ___ nc ___
4. w ___ rk
5. m ___ m ___ nt
6. sch ___ ___ l
7. d ___ ff ___ r ___ nt

Sight Words

morning
once
work
school

Story Words

moment
different
country

B. Draw a line to match each word with the clue for it.

8. moment   a. the first part of the day
9. different   b. a very short time
10. morning   c. not alike

Unit 6

Phonics

A. Circle the word that has the same *middle* sound as the picture.

1.   farm   cork   car

2.   corn   stone   want

3.   stay   blond   floor

4.   soap   score   son

B. Draw a line to the word that names the picture.

5.   store

6.   corn

7.   score

8.   floor

Name _____ Date _____

Unit 6
Reading 3

Think It Over

Reread to tell about the story.

In the morning, Star reads in her classroom at school. Star likes to share her books with her friends.

Carl likes to eat lunch with his friends. Carl has fun throughout the day.

A. Circle the letter of the right answer. Then write the word.

1. In the morning, Star _____.
   - a. writes
   - b. plays
   - c. reads
   - d. cleans up

2. Star likes to share her _____.
   - a. snack
   - b. pencils
   - c. toys
   - d. books

3. Carl likes to eat lunch with his _____.
   - a. friends
   - b. teachers
   - c. family
   - d. teammates

Unit 6

B. Fill in the diagram to compare and contrast your morning with Star's morning. Put things that are the same in the middle. Put things that are different on one side or the other.

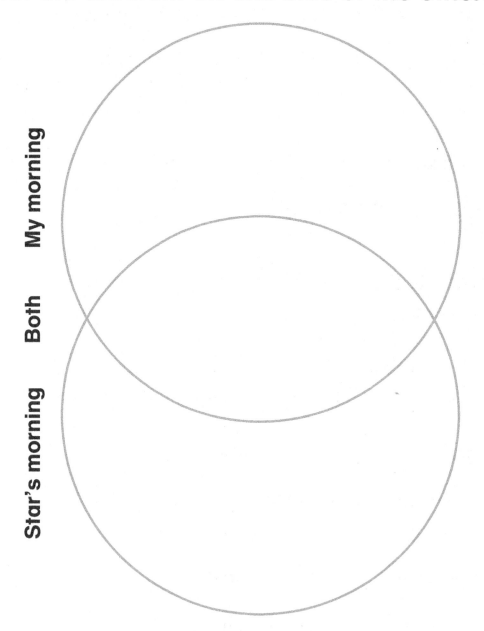

148

Name _____ Date _____

Grammar and Writing

Adverbs of Time

> Use adverbs and prepositions of time such as **before**, **after**, **in**, **on**, and **at** to tell when something happens.
>
> Use **first**, **then**, **next**, and **finally** to show the order in which things happen.

A. Complete the sentences with the correct prepositions from the box.

in
after
on
at
before

1. The game is <u>on</u> Saturday.

2. Let's go to the park _____ we finish school.

3. My father's birthday is _____ October.

4. We eat lunch _____ 12:00.

5. I brush my teeth _____ I go to bed.

6. I have chocolate cake _____ my birthday.

149

Unit 6

B. Complete the paragraph with *Finally*, *Then*, *First*, or *Next*. Use a comma (,) where needed.

This is what I do every night: _____ I eat dinner with my family. _____ I do my homework. _____ I watch TV. _____ I brush my teeth. _____ I go to bed.

Write

Complete the paragraph with information about what you do every day in the morning. Use *before* and *after* and prepositions.

　　This is what I do every morning before I go to school:

I wake up _____

_____

_____

Name _____ Date _____

Review

Answer the questions after reading Unit 6. You can go back and reread to help find the answers.

1. Circle all the words with the *ir*, *ur*, and *er* sounds.

   > Every Saturday, Anh comes to my house to play and eat dinner.

2. What does Bea eat at Anh's house? Circle the letter of the correct answer.
   - **a.** chocolate cake
   - **b.** noodle soup
   - **c.** warm bread
   - **d.** fruit

3. In *Schools Around the World*, how can this class learn more about students from around the world?

   _____
   _____

4. In *Time at School and at Home*, where does Star live? Circle the letter of the correct answer.
   - **a.** Argentina
   - **b.** Nairobi
   - **c.** United States
   - **d.** Germany

Unit 6

5. In *Time at School and at Home*, why do you think Dar had a long day?

_____

_____

6. Circle all the words with the *ar* sound.

> My name is Mark. This is Star. This is a boy named Carl. Jane and her dad visit a big park.

7. Circle all the words with the *or/ore* sound.

> This morning, the class would like to learn more about students from around the world.

8. What country from this unit would you like to visit? What are two foods you would like to try from this country?

_____

_____

_____

_____

Name _____ Date _____

Writing Workshop
Write a How-to Paragraph

Write a paragraph explaining how to do something.

1. **Prewrite** Plan your paragraph. Write the steps in the graphic organizer below. Make sure they are in the correct order.

Step 1
Step 2
Step 3
Step 4
Step 5

Unit 6

Unit 6

2. **Draft** Use your graphic organizer to write a first draft.

_____

3. **Revise** Read your draft. Does it explain how to do something? Try to write better sentences.

4. **Edit** Use the Editing Checklist on page 346 of your book to check your paragraph. Correct your writing.

5. **Publish** Make a clean copy of your final draft on a sheet of paper. Share it with the class.

Name _____ Date _____

Unit 6

Fluency

A. Read the sentences aloud. Practice saying them as fast as you can with no mistakes.

1. In the snowy winter sun,

    Sally sunburned—not much fun.

2. On the farm or at the park,

    get home safe before it's dark.

5. Thunder, lightning—what a storm!

    Behind our door we're safe and warm.

B. Read each sentence several times. Then cover each one with your hand and try to say it word for word.

1. Peter found a bird's nest in the dirt.

2. Globes and maps show the Arctic circle.

3. At the shore, people swim and play in the sand.

Unit 6

C. Take turns reading the sentences aloud with a partner. Use your finger to follow the words. Read aloud for one minute. Count your words.

"Schools Around the World" tells what it is like for	10
students in their schools and homes. Chun	17
is from China. He works hard in school and	26
helps his mom and dad at home. Ande is from	36
Kenya, and he likes school work better than	44
his chores. Marco is from Brazil. The hot sun	53
shines, the palm trees grow, and Marco plays	61
on the shore. The students learn about each	69
other.	70

D. Read to your teacher, friends, or family.

Name _____ Date _____

Unit 6

Learning Checklist

Word Study and Phonics

- ☐ Suffixes
- ☐ *R* Controlled Vowels: *ir, er, ur*
- ☐ *R* Controlled Vowel: *ar*
- ☐ *R* Controlled Vowels: *or, ore*

Reading Strategies

- ☐ Use Visuals
- ☐ Main Idea and Details
- ☐ Make Connections

Grammar

- ☐ Infinitive
- ☐ Capitalization
- ☐ Adverbs of Time

Writing

- ☐ Write about what you want to do when you grow up.
- ☐ Write about a country.
- ☐ Explain what happens on a typical school day.
- ☐ Writing Workshop: Write a How-To Paragraph

Listening and Speaking

- ☐ Demonstration